Cobán Treasure Hunt

by
WES EBY

BEACON HILL PRESS
OF KANSAS CITY

Copyright 2010
by Beacon Hill Press of Kansas City

Printed in the United States of America

ISBN 978-0-8341-2489-9

Cover Design: Doug Bennett
Interior Design: Sharon Page
Illustrator: Lon Eric Craven

Editor: Donna Manning
Assistant Editor: Laura S. Lohberger

Note: This story is based on the Nazarene mission work in Guatemala. It includes factual information about the following: the missionary work of Richard and Anna Maude Anderson, the Alabaster celebration at Cobán, and the Bible school in Cobán where the first Alabaster building was built. This book is part of the *Kidz Passport to Missions* curriculum.

10 9 8 7 6 5 4 3 2 1

Dedication

To my sons—
Ed, Joe, Rob, and Dan—
and their families.

With love,
Dad and Grandpa

Contents

1
The Computer Crash

"Mom, come here!" Candy yelled in anger.

"What is it?" her mother asked, as she hurried into the living room.

"This stupid computer just quit working," Candy complained, slamming her fist on the computer desk.

"Calm down, Candy," her mother said. "Your anger will not fix the computer."

"But I can't email Hannah," the 11-year-old cried. "I promised to write her today."

"Let me see if I can find out what's wrong," Mrs. Caine said. She sat down at the desk and clicked on the start tab.

"I'm going outside to see what Timmy is doing," Candy said. She headed for the front door with her fists still clinched.

"OK," Mother said. "Don't stay too long. Lunch will be . . ." Candy was gone before her mother finished the sentence.

Candy's parents, Jason and Emma Caine, had been missionaries in Guatemala [GWAH-tuh-MAH-luh] for 12 years. Rev. Caine taught at the Nazarene seminary, and his wife worked with compassionate ministries. Their two children, Candice and Timothy, were born in Guatemala and enjoyed the life of adventure in this Central American country.

Candice, usually called Candy by her parents, was an outgoing girl with short brown hair and bright green eyes with long lashes. She was full of energy and loved to stay busy. She worked on the computer, played soccer, explored new places, and made scrapbooks. Timothy, or Timmy, captured people with his innocent face and blond buzz cut. He stood out among the darker-skinned people in Guatemala. He was energetic and loved to compete with his sister.

Fifteen minutes later, Candy ran back into the house. "Mom, I'm never going outside again," she said as she stomped her feet. "Those kids keep teasing me. They're *so* mean."

"What's wrong now?" her mother asked.

"They called me 'Candy Cane,' and it makes me so angry. They chanted, 'Candy Cane, Candy Cane, do you have a candy brain?'"

Mrs. Caine put her arm around her daughter's shoulder. "My dear, it doesn't feel good when people make fun of you. They do it because they know you'll get angry."

"But they know I don't like it," Candy said. "They're just awful!"

"I know they aren't very kind. You just need to walk away, and they may stop teasing you."

"I don't think they'll ever stop," Candy declared. She stood with her hands on her hips as if she knew exactly what her teasers would do.

"What do you think Jesus would do?" Mrs. Caine asked. "Don't you think He prayed for the people who mistreated Him?"

"Well, maybe," Candy said. She bowed her head and looked at the floor.

"Just think about what I said. Would you let me pray with you?"

"OK," Candy said without looking up at her mother.

"Our Father, I pray today for Candy and the problem she has with anger. I know that You love her and want to help her. Please help her control her anger when others tease her. Help Candy to show them Your love by the way she acts and what she says. Then she can be a witness for You to the children in our neighborhood. We pray in Jesus' name. Amen."

"Thanks, Mom," Candy said softly, as she wiped tears from her eyes. "I'm sorry I get so angry. I want Jesus to help me."

"Jesus *will* help you. He promised that He would. I want to help you too. Will you let me?"

"I guess. What do you mean?"

"Every time you get angry and upset," her mother said, "I will make the letter 'J' with my right hand, or I will just say 'J.' What do you think that means?"

"I . . . I don't know," Candy said.

"Who did we just talk about?" Mrs. Caine asked. "Who can help you with your anger problem?"

"Jesus," Candy said with a hint of a smile.

"Exactly. And when I make or say the letter 'J,' this will remind you to ask Jesus to help you. This will be our secret code, OK?"

"That's cool, Mom. I *will* remember. And I won't tell anyone else."

* * *

"Hey, Mom, can I play a computer game?" Timmy said, as he ran into the house.

"No, you can't!" his sister exclaimed. "The dumb computer is broken!" She kicked her leg toward the desk as if she wanted to destroy the machine.

"Candy, remember 'J'?" her mother said as she made the letter "J" with a finger and thumb.

Candy lowered her head. "I'm sorry, Mom. I'm trying to remember."

"OK. I'll remind you. Every day if I have to."

"Hey, what's this 'J' thing?" Timmy asked.

"It's a secret between Candy and me," his mother answered. "I would be happy if you didn't ask about it again."

"What's wrong with the computer?" Timmy asked.

"I don't know," Mother replied. "I couldn't find the problem. We'll check it out this evening when your father comes home."

"What am I going to do?" Timmy asked. "No computer. No school. It's so boring around here."

"Bored already? You've only been out of school for one week," Mother said. "But I've got an idea that I'll tell you about tomorrow."

"Why tomorrow?" Timmy asked.

"Why not now?" Candy insisted.

"I need to talk with your father first. I think you'll like what we plan to tell you."

"I can't wait!" Timmy said. He jumped up and down as only an eight-year-old can do.

"Cool!" Candy added. "This is like Christmas."

"And candy canes are a Christmas treat," Mother said with a wink aimed at her daughter.

Candy smiled. "Yep, candy canes are a real sweet treat."

2
The Treasure Hunt Plans

"Ready for flapjacks?" Mrs. Caine asked, as she placed a huge platter of pancakes on the kitchen table.

"Sure. I could eat all of them," Timmy said, bouncing in his chair.

"Well, maybe you could," his father said with a chuckle. "But I suggest you start with two, and if you want more, you can have them."

Flapjacks were the favorite breakfast for the Caine family. They enjoyed them at least twice a week. After Timmy said grace, the entire family tackled the pile of pancakes.

"Hey, Mom," Candy said, "you promised to tell us something special today. Remember?"

"That's right," Timmy said. "Tell us now."

"I did promise you, didn't I?" Mother said. "Jason, why don't you tell them."

"Sure," Father agreed. "I'm going to our Bible school in Cobán [koh-BAHN] next week to teach some courses for the pastors. Since I'll be gone for four weeks, I've arranged for all of you to go with me."

"That's cool!" Candy said.

"Yippee!" Timmy yelled. "Where is Cobán?"

"About 130 miles north of Guatemala City up in the mountains," Father answered. "It's the place where Nazarene mission work started in this country."

"Will we be back before Thanksgiving?" Timmy asked.

"Yes, we'll be back the week before the holiday."

In Guatemala, children go to school from January through September. Their school vacation is October through December.

"Why did missionaries go to Cobán?" Candy asked.

"A good question," Rev. Caine said. "The first missionaries settled on the seacoast, but many of them became very sick. There were lots of mosquitoes. The bite of these insects caused people to become ill with malaria and yellow fever. A few missionaries died, and others returned home. So the missionaries looked for a place with no mosquitoes. The mountains seemed to be the perfect spot."

"I can't wait to go," Timmy said, as he took a big bite of pancake. "But where will we live?"

"In an apartment at the Bible school."

"What will we do while you're teaching, Dad?" Candy asked.

"I have a great idea," Mother answered. "I'm planning a treasure hunt that will take you around Cobán."

"Super!" Candy exclaimed. "That's so cool."

"I love treasure hunts," Timmy said.

"Every few days I'll give you a clue to help you find the next treasure," Mother said. "At the end of the hunt, you'll find a *special* treasure. As you're searching for that special treasure, I hope you'll learn some things that are very important."

"What's that, Mom?" Candy asked.

"I won't tell you that right now."

"Oh, come on, Mom," Candy said. "Please tell us."

"If I told you now, it would spoil some of the fun of the treasure hunt. You need to be surprised."

"You can start packing your suitcases today, if you want," Dad said. "Be sure to take your rain ponchos. We're packing our raincoats and umbrellas. It rains a lot up there."

"Another pancake, Timmy?" Mother asked. "There are two left."

"No, thanks," he answered. "I'm stuffed just like a big turkey."

"What about eating the whole platter?" Father teased. He chuckled as he patted Timmy on the head.

"I want to start packing now," Timmy said. "May I be excused?"

"Me too?" Candy asked.

"Sure, kids, go for it!"

✳ ✳ ✳

The following week, the Caines packed their Honda and headed to Cobán. The paved road from Guatemala City carved its way up and down through the mountains. It passed lush plants, tall trees, gorgeous flowers, and abundant crops. Candy and Timmy gazed out the windows, eagerly looking for what was new around the next sharp curve.

"Watch out, Dad!" Candy hollered. "Look at that drop-off!"

"I see it," he replied. "I'm driving as carefully as I can. I know this road doesn't have many guardrails."

"With all these curves and drop-offs, it almost makes me dizzy."

"I like this road," Timmy said. "It's like the roller coaster at Disney World."

"Look, kids," their father said, "there's a sign for the Church of the Nazarene."

"Neat," Candy said. "Will we see more signs?"

"A lot more," he answered. "Why don't you count them and see how many there are before we reach Cobán?"

"OK," Candy said.

"Sis, I'll count them too," Timmy said.

The Caines rode in silence for a time as the highway took them up and down and around and around.

"There's another sign," Candy said. "See, Dad?"

"I see it too," said Timmy.

As the family climbed higher and higher up the mountain, the children kept counting the church signs. Three. Four. Five. Soon they were up to 14. They also passed many small booths beside the road where the local people sold vegetables and fruit from their gardens.

"I'm thirsty," Timmy said. "Can we get something to drink?"

"That's a good idea, Son," Father said. "We'll see if they have Cokes at the next booth."

"Cool," Candy said. "I want an orange soda."

There was barely enough room to park the car at the roadside booth.

"Jason, are you sure we're far enough off the road?" Emma asked. "We don't want anyone to hit our car."

"Well, I can't get any closer without hitting the booth," Dad said with a chuckle. "Let's get our drinks and hurry on our way."

Rev. Caine asked the owner what drinks he had. The man said he had only Coke and Sprite.

"But I wanted an orange soda!" Candy yelled, as she kicked the front of the roadside booth. "Why don't you have orange soda?"

"Candice," her father said sternly. Her parents usually called her Candice when they were upset with her. "You must apologize to this nice man."

"Remember 'J'?" her mother added.

"I'm sorry," Candy said quietly to the owner.

Candy and Timmy each bought a Coke, and their parents got Sprite. The family got into their Honda and continued the trip to Cobán.

After several minutes, it began to get darker.

"Whoa," Rev. Caine said. "I'd better slow down."

"Why is there fog this high in the mountains?" Candy asked.

"This fog is actually a cloud," Dad answered.

"A cloud?" Candy and Timmy asked at the same time.

"That's right. Fog is a cloud that touches the ground. This sometimes happens on the road to Cobán. When the clouds are down low, we drive right through them."

"Cool!" Candy said. "I can't wait to email my friend Hannah and tell her."

Suddenly, the cloud disappeared.

"Look, Dad," Timmy said. "There's another church sign."

"How many have you counted so far?" Father asked.

"We've counted 23," Candy said. "There are lots of Nazarene churches up here."

"Yes, there are many churches in this area," Rev. Caine said. "Most towns and villages have at least one Church of the Nazarene."

"We'll have lots of fun in Cobán," Candy said.

"Can't you drive faster, Dad?" Timmy asked.

As the Honda rounded another curve, Cobán was just ahead.

"We're almost there," Mrs. Caine said. "Kids, are you ready for the Cobán treasure hunt?"

3
The Mystery Envelope

"I want this room," Timmy said, as he pointed out the window. "Look, see the men playing soccer?"

"Why can't I have this room?" Candy asked. She stormed into the bedroom, stomped her feet, and kicked the leg of a chair, knocking it over. "You always get the best room, Timmy. You aren't the only one in this family who plays soccer, you know. You are nothing but a spoiled, little brat!"

"Candice," her mother said, as she walked into the room. "Remember . . ."

"I know, I know, remember 'J'," Candy mocked as she interrupted her mother. "I'm tired of remembering 'J'! I'm sick and tired of it!" She stomped her foot several times as she spoke.

"Please, come with me," her mother said firmly. "We need to have a talk."

"Do I *really* have to?" Candy whined.

Her mother didn't answer but gave her one of those you-better-obey-me looks. Before Candy left the room, she looked back at her brother and stuck out her tongue at him. Then she followed her mother to the kitchen, where Mrs. Caine sat down at a small, round table.

"Sit down, dear," Candy's mother said. When Candy hesitated, her mother said sternly, "Now!"

As Candy pulled out a chair, the back legs scraped the floor and made two long black marks on the tile. She plopped down, folded her arms, and sent a glare to her mother.

"Your anger is not getting any better," Mrs. Caine began. "What you said to your brother was unkind. And your actions just now make me sad. If your father had seen you, he would have been so disappointed. And I know that Jesus is not pleased. We have just arrived in Cobán, and if you don't control your anger, none of us will enjoy our time here. What do you think we should do?"

Candy shrugged her shoulders. By this time, she no longer glared. "Mom, I'm sorry. I really am. I don't know why I get so angry. I do want Jesus to help me."

"Why don't we pray again and ask Jesus to help you control your anger?" She reached out and held her daughter's hands. As her mother prayed, Candy's eyes filled with tears. By the time her mother said amen, Candy was weeping.

"Now, Candy, you need to pray too," her mother said softly.

"I'll try," Candy said. Between sobs, she prayed, "Dear Jesus, I'm sorry that I get so angry. Please forgive me. Help me to be kind to Timmy, and to Mom and Dad too. I really mean it. Amen."

"That was a nice prayer," her mother said, "and I think you *do* mean it. Now, what should you do right now?"

"I guess I should apologize to Timmy."

"That's a good start," her mother said. "And what else?"

"I don't know."

"What about the kitchen floor?"

"Oh," Candy said, as she looked at the tile. "I need to clean these black marks."

"That's right," Mrs. Caine said. "After all, you did make them, and this is not our house."

"OK. I'll talk to Timmy first, and then I'll work on the floor."

Candy hurried to find her brother, who was still in the bedroom looking out the window. "Timmy, you can have this bedroom," she said. "I'm sorry I called you a name and made a face at you."

"That's OK, Sis. Maybe Mom will let us switch bedrooms in a couple weeks."

"Thanks, Timmy. You are a good little brother." Candy turned around and ran to the kitchen to work on the black marks.

Twenty minutes later, Rev. Caine entered the apartment to find Candy on her hands and knees, scrubbing the kitchen floor.

"Candy, I'm glad to see you're working already. When you're finished, I want you and Timmy to help me with the suitcases. There are also sacks of food, lots of bedding, and a couple of boxes of your stuff to unload."

"Sure, Dad," she said. "I'm almost done."

Shortly, the children joined their father outside. In just a few minutes, the car was unloaded.

"Dad, may I go watch the soccer game?" Candy asked. "I won't stay long."

"Yes, and why don't you take Timmy with you? But I want both of you back in 30 minutes so you can unpack your suitcases before supper."

"Thanks, Dad," Candy said as she ran out the door. Timmy was right on her heels. "We'll be back on time."

Thirty minutes passed. Then forty. "I wonder why the kids have not returned," Mr. Caine said to his wife. "I told them to be back here in . . ."

Just then, Timmy came flying into the house. "Dad, Mom, come quick! Something bad has happened to Candy." The boy sobbed as he spoke.

"What happened?" Dad asked, as he stooped down in front of his son.

Through his tears, Timmy answered, "Candy is bleeding. A soccer ball hit her."

Rev. Caine took his son's hand as they hurried out the door. Mrs. Caine grabbed two towels and followed them. They ran to the sports field where Candy was lying on a small wooden bench, surrounded by soccer players.

"We've stopped the bleeding," one of the soccer players said, "but I think her nose is broken."

"Let me have a look," Mrs. Caine said. She used the towels to wipe the blood from her daughter's face. "There's a gash on her nose," she said, "but I think she'll be OK. I have some medicine and bandages at the apartment, and that should take care of the cut."

Candy's father and one of the soccer players made a seat by crossing their arms; then they carried her to the apartment. As they walked, Rev. Caine introduced himself and his family. "We will be here for a month, and I'll teach a couple of classes at the Bible school."

"I'm Antonio Vega [ahn-TOH-nee-oh VAY-guh], but most people call me Tony," the soccer player said. "I'll be one of your students. I'm glad to meet you, Professor Caine, but I wish it had been in the classroom. I kicked the soccer ball that hit your daughter. I didn't mean to hurt her."

"It's not your fault, Tony. It was an accident," Rev. Caine said. "I'm sure Candy will be fine."

"I'll be OK," Candy said. "I'm just glad you got the bleeding to stop."

"You're a good sport," Tony said. "Some people would be angry with me."

"Well, I wanted to," Candy admitted, "but I prayed for Jesus to help me. And He did."

"I'm so proud of you, dear," Mrs. Caine said. "Really proud."

✳ ✳ ✳

"I wish the rain would stop," Candy said. "I want to go exploring."

"I want to play soccer," Timmy said. "I could wear my rain poncho, couldn't I?"

Mother laughed. "How did you come up with that idea? What a smart son I have." She winked as she looked at Timmy, who returned her smile with a big grin.

Candy and Timmy were eating black beans and eggs with tortillas, a typical breakfast in Guatemala. Their mother was washing dishes.

"After breakfast, I want to check your nose," Mother said. "Your face is still swollen, and you'll be black and blue for several days. How are you feeling?"

"I'm OK," Candy said. "My nose still hurts. I'll be glad when I look normal again."

"What can we do today?" Timmy asked.

"Since it's raining, why don't you work in your bed-rooms?"

"What about the treasure hunt you promised?" Candy asked.

"Yeah, what about the treasure hunt?" Timmy imitated his big sister.

"Well, if it doesn't rain tomorrow," Mother said, "you can begin the treasure hunt. Before you go to bed tonight, I'll give you the first clue."

"Yippee!" Timmy yelled.

"I can't wait," Candy said.

* * *

"I'm glad my bedroom has a desk," Candy said. "I can work on my scrapbook while I'm here. Right, Mom?"

"You can if you brought your box of photos and postcards."

"They're right here," Candy said, as she put the box on the desk.

Mrs. Caine looked around the room. "Timmy doesn't have a desk like this."

"I know. This desk is great. I think I'll keep this room the whole time we're here."

Mother and daughter worked for several minutes. Suddenly, Candy said, "Mom, what's this?" She held up an envelope. "It was in the bottom desk drawer."

Mrs. Caine took the sealed envelope from her daughter and looked at both sides. "There's a message in Spanish on the back side of the envelope. You read it, Candy."

"Open only in case of an emergency," she read. "This is a real mystery. What emergency could it mean?"

4

The Treasure Hunt Begins

After dinner that evening, Candy and Timmy could hardly sit still.

"Calm down, Timmy," his father said. "You're going to wear a hole in the couch the way you bounce up and down."

"I'm too excited, Dad," he said.

Candy smiled. "We're ready, Mom. Please give us our first clue to the treasure hunt."

"OK, but you have to promise one thing," Mother said.

"We promise. Don't we, Timmy?"

"Yep. Anything, Mom."

"You cannot stay up past nine o'clock trying to figure out the clue. Lights out at nine."

"I promise," both kids said in unison.

"The clue is written on a card inside this envelope," Mother said, as she handed it to the children.

Timmy opened the envelope and handed the card to Candy, who read the clue out loud.

Clue 1
To solve this clue, you must be brave,
For it will be beside a grave.
To solve this clue you won't be done,
Till you find the name of Anderson.

"This is a mystery, like the envelope I found in my desk," Candy said. "Mom, have you told Dad about it?"

"Oh, I had forgotten about it." Mrs. Caine went to the kitchen, opened a cabinet, got the envelope, and gave it to her husband.

"I found this in my desk today," Candy explained. "It says to open only in case of an emergency. What does this mean, Dad?"

"Hmm, let me think about it," he answered. He turned the envelope over, and then turned it upside down. "I won't open it now. I'll sleep on it."

"Don't hurt it," Candy said with a laugh. Her parents smiled at her joke.

Timmy looked puzzled. "What does that mean?" he asked.

"Dad said that he would 'sleep on it,'" Candy said. "That means he wants to think about it some more before he does anything. But if you sleep on something, like a kitten, you could hurt it. So I told him not to hurt it, and . . ."

"I get it, I get it," Timmy said with a laugh.

"This clue is hard." Candy looked at the card again. "Anderson? I wonder who Anderson is. Won't you give us a hint?"

"Not now," Mrs. Caine said. "Why don't we play a game before bedtime? What would you like to play?"

"Mexican Train," Timmy said.

"Yes, that's lots of fun," Candy agreed.

"I'll get the dominoes," Rev. Caine said. "I put them in our bedroom closet."

For the next hour and a half, the Caine family played several rounds of their favorite table game.

"What's the score?" Candy asked before the last round.

"You have 180," her mother said, who kept the score. "Your father has 296. I have 173, and Timmy has 168. It appears that your father will lose this game. But Candy, it's possible for you, Timmy, or me to win."

"Even though Timmy is ahead, I can still beat him," Candy said.

After the final round, Timmy had the lowest score. "OK, Timmy, you won tonight," Candy said. "But I'll get you the next time."

"I'm so proud of you, Candy," Mother said. "You weren't angry when you didn't win the game."

"I pray every day that Jesus will help me," she said, "and He is helping me, Mom."

"I'm proud of you too," Father said, as he hugged Candy. "Now, let's pray before you go to bed."

After their prayer time, the kids hugged and kissed their parents good-night.

"Remember, lights out at nine," Mom reminded them. "Sleep tight."

"And don't let the bedbugs bite," Timmy added.

"And if they do, then be polite," Candy joked.

Everyone laughed as the children hurried off to their bedrooms.

✳ ✳ ✳

The next day, the Cobán sun shone brightly.

"Yippee!" Timmy squealed. "No rain!"

"We're going on a treasure hunt. We're going on a treasure hunt," Candy chanted.

Timmy picked up the chant and they repeated it together. "We're going on a treasure hunt. We're going on a treasure hunt."

"Enough of that, kids," Mother said with a smile. "Finish your breakfast, please."

Breakfast for Candy and Timmy was Cheerios, orange juice, and fried plantain. Plantains are a popular food in Guatemala. While they look like bananas, their skin is green, and they are usually cooked before people eat them.

"Do you know who Anderson is?" Timmy asked.

"No, I'm puzzled about that," his sister answered. "I have no idea. Mom, are you going to tell us?"

"Not right now," she replied. "I want you to think about the clues."

"I've been thinking hard. I even dreamed about it." Then Candy asked, "When are we going?"

"After lunch. This morning I have some work to do for your father. You and your brother can play in your rooms or go outside. But you are not to leave the yard."

"All right, Mom," she said. "See if Dad knows anything about our mystery envelope."

"By the way," Mother asked, "does your nose still hurt?"

"A little," Candy answered. "I wish the black and blue would go away. I'm tired of looking this way."

"I know, dear."

"It will be better soon, won't it?"

"I sure hope so. I know you are miserable."

✳ ✳ ✳

"Kids, are you ready to go treasure hunting?" Mrs. Caine asked after lunch.

"You bet!" Timmy said, as he jumped up and down.

"Ready?" Candy replied. "I was ready before we ever came to Cobán."

"We'll talk about the clue as we go," their mother said. "Where do you think we're going?"

"Well," said Candy, "I think it's a cemetery."

"Why?" asked Timmy.

"The clue says 'beside a grave,' and the only graves I know about are in a cemetery."

"Right you are," her mother said. "So, we'll go to a cemetery here in Cobán. What else does the clue tell you?"

"Find the grave of a person by the name of Anderson." Candy spoke with confidence.

"You are a good detective," her mother said. "That's the way to solve the mystery."

After a 20-minute ride in their Honda, they arrived at the cemetery. Mrs. Caine parked the car just inside the gate. "There are lots of graves in this cemetery," she said. "So you need to look for the right grave."

"With the name Anderson on the grave marker, Timmy," Candy said in a big sister kind of way.

The two children spent the next 15 minutes running from grave to grave. Finally, Timmy shouted, "Here it is!"

When Candy and Mrs. Caine looked at the grave marker, Candy said, "False alarm. This isn't Anderson. It says Roberto [roh-BAIR-toh]."

Mrs. Caine read the name on the grave marker, "Roberto Arriaga [ah-ree-AH-gah]. This man was from Guatemala."

Candy and Timmy continued running from grave to grave. Soon they were huffing and puffing. Candy stopped to catch her breath. "This cemetery has lots of hills."

"I think they are mountains," Timmy said. "Big mountains!"

"We *are* in the mountains," their mother observed. "You can walk instead of run, you know."

After a few more minutes, Timmy shouted, "Come here! I think I found it."

When Mrs. Caine arrived at the grave, she said, "Another false alarm. This is where Juan Alvarado [WAHN ahl-vah-RAH-doh] is buried. You need to look some more."

The children walked up and down the cemetery hills.

"Here it is!" Candy hollered. "I found it!"

Her mother and brother hurried to the grave, and there it was: Richard S. Anderson.

"Mom, who is Richard Anderson?" Candy asked. "Anderson is not a Spanish name."

"You're right. He was from the United States, not Guatemala. Rev. Anderson and his wife, Anna Maude, were two of the early Nazarene missionaries to Guatemala. At first, they lived on the seacoast, but they almost died from yellow fever. So they moved to Cobán where the climate is more healthy. What is the date on the grave marker?"

The children looked closely at the date that was almost worn away. "It says 1945," Candy said.

"That's right. He lived here for more than 40 years. One of the important things he did was to print literature in the language the people could read. That literature was considered a precious treasure. When Rev. Anderson died, he was buried right here in Cobán."

"A treasure?" Candy asked. "Books and stuff would not be a treasure to me."

"But think about it," her mother said. "If you did not have anything to read, how would you feel? What if you did not have a Bible or Sunday School literature or

31

any books? Wouldn't you appreciate it if suddenly you had something to read?"

"Yes, I see what you mean," Candy answered. "Books and other stuff would seem like a treasure."

"Look around and see if you can find another clue," encouraged Mother.

The children looked under several rocks and in the grass. Finally, Timmy looked in a flower vase. "There's an envelope down in this vase," he said. "This must be it." He pulled it out and handed it to Candy. "Here, Sis."

Candy opened the envelope and read the clue, stumbling over three of the words.

Clue 2
To solve this clue, you go to town,
On Calle Kekchi [KAH-yeh KEK-chee] look around.
This clue will not be easily seen
Because it's down in java beans.

5

The Treasure Hunt Goes On

After dinner that evening, the Caine family settled down in the living room, each one with a book. Rev. Caine read a textbook for one of his classes. Timmy had fallen asleep, and his book was on the floor. Although Candy was awake, she could not concentrate on her story.

"Mom, when are you going to help us with our new clue?" Candy asked.

"When you really need the help," she answered.

"But all I can think about is that clue," Candy said.

"I know, dear," her mother said, "but I want you to use your gray matter."

"What's 'gray matter'?" Candy wanted to know.

"Good question," Dad said. "Why don't you look it up?"

"We don't have a dictionary," Candy whined.

"Well, I'll go to the school and borrow one." Rev. Caine quickly left the house and jogged over to the classroom building.

"Your father is right," Mother said. "When you don't know a word, it's a good idea to look it up. That will also help you with the treasure hunt clue. Look up the words you don't know."

Rev. Caine returned with a dictionary. "Here you are, Candy. Now look up 'gray matter.'"

Candy found the "G" words right away and turned a few pages until she found the term. "Gray matter," she read, "is brownish-gray nerve tissue, especially of the brain, made up of nerve cell bodies." She stopped. "This is hard. It says, 'brain,' so it must have something to do with the brain."

"You're exactly right," her mother said. "Does the dictionary say anything else?"

Candy looked at the dictionary again and read aloud, "'Brains, intellect.' So, I *am* right. 'Gray matter' means the brain."

Mother nodded. "So, when I said I want you to use your gray matter, what did I mean?"

"I get it," Candy replied. "You want me to use my brain."

"Now, use your brain to figure out the clue you have," her mother said. "What words don't you know?"

"Well, 'java' for one," Candy answered. "I'll look it up in the dictionary."

Candy turned to the "J" words and found "java." "It says that Java is an island in Indonesia [in-duh-NEE-zhuh] and is capitalized."

"Keep reading," her mother urged.

"Oh, I see. The next definition is 'coffee.' Java beans are coffee beans."

"Isn't this fun?" her father said. "When you take time to learn something new, it's rewarding."

Mother continued to prod them. "What else don't you know about the clue?"

"The words 'C-a-l-l-e K-e-k-c-h-i,'" Candy said as she spelled them. "I don't even know how to say them."

"The second word is the name of some people who live here in the mountains of central Guatemala. Their name is pronounced 'KEK-chee' and rhymes with 'peck me.'"

"I'll remember that word now," Candy said. "But what about the other word?"

"You know Spanish," her mother replied. "You've seen that word many times in Guatemala City on road signs."

"Oh, it means 'street.'" Candy looked at her mother. "Doesn't it?"

"Right," her mother responded. "That's using your gray matter, dear."

"The clue says we have to go to town and look around on Calle Kekchi," Candy said. "And we have to look for another clue in coffee beans?"

"Exactly," Mother said. "Great work, Candy."

Her father closed his book and said, "You're using your noggin."

"Now, Dad," Candy said, as she rolled her eyes. "I suppose you want me to look up that word too?"

"How did you ever guess?" he answered with a chuckle.

"OK, OK." Candy picked up the dictionary and turned to the "N" pages. She located the word and read aloud, "a small mug or cup."

Without looking up, she said, "That doesn't make sense."

"Keep reading," her dad said. "You'll find it."

Candy looked at the dictionary again and read, "A person's head. Now I get it. 'Noggin' means head, and you want me to use the gray matter inside my noggin."

"Bravo!" her father said. Both Mom and Dad clapped their hands at their daughter's discovery.

The clapping awakened Timmy, who rubbed his eyes and asked, "What's happening? What have I missed?"

"The answer to the clue," his sister said. "That's all."

"When are we going to go find it?" he asked.

"Not tonight," his mother said, as she hugged him. "It's time for bed now. We'll go when we have another sunny day."

"I'll tell you about the clue tomorrow," Candy said. "This hunt will be fun, and this time it's *not* in the cemetery."

* * *

"It's rained for three days. When is it going to stop?" Candy asked.

"Who knows?" Mother answered. "It can rain for a week or more at a time."

"We'll never find the next clue," Candy complained. "I'm so tired of the rain."

"Can't we go anyway?" Timmy asked.

"We have our ponchos," Candy added. "Why can't we, Mom?"

"I don't know my way around Cobán well enough to drive in bad weather," she said. "I think we need to wait and see what happens tomorrow."

"I'm praying for sunshine," Candy said. "Lots of sunshine!"

* * *

"Yippee!" Timmy yelled when he jumped out of bed the next morning. He ran to the kitchen. "Mom, look, it's stopped raining."

"I know, son," his mother replied. "I'm glad too."

"We can go treasure hunting," Candy added. "I can't wait!"

"After you kids eat breakfast, we'll go on our next search."

Candy and Timmy gobbled their breakfast and then jumped in the car. They were ready for the day's adventure.

"Where are we going?" Timmy asked.

His mother responded, "Candy, can you tell him?"

"Well, the clue says Calle Kekchi, so we need to find a street named Kekchi," explained Candy. "And we need to find some java beans. That's coffee beans, Timmy."

"Yippee!" exclaimed Timmy. "We're going to a store."

"Where else would you find coffee beans?" Mother asked.

"On a coffee farm?" Candy was unsure of her answer.

"Well, yes," her mother replied, "that's a good answer. Sometimes they are called coffee plantations. There are coffee plantations all around this part of Guatemala. But that's not where we're going today."

"Then where are we going?" Candy wanted to know.

"Just wait. We'll be there soon."

The children pressed their faces against the car windows and looked out. They saw small houses with flowers in front, people in colorful clothes, and women with baskets on their heads.

"There it is!" Candy shouted. She pointed to the left side of the road. "The sign says 'Calle Kekchi.'"

"I don't see a store," Timmy said.

"Keep looking," Mother instructed.

In a few minutes, Mrs. Caine parked the car, and the kids jumped out of the Honda.

"See the market ahead?" Mom said, as she pointed down the street. "There are lots of booths in the market, and the people sell all types of food and other things. You need to find a booth that sells java beans. Somewhere in the java beans you will find the next clue and the treasure."

"Let's go!" Candy started to run.

"Wait for me," Timmy called to his big sister.

"Whoa," Mother said. "We have plenty of time. I want you to stay near me. OK?"

"OK. But hurry up." Candy was impatient.

"You'll have to slow down, kids," Mom said, catching her breath. "I can't keep up with you."

Soon they passed several market booths where they saw clothing, dolls, jewelry, and items made of leather. But no coffee beans. A block later, they came to booths that sold produce, bread, drinks, and meat.

A few minutes later, Candy pointed to a large burlap sack. "Mother, aren't these java beans?"

"Yes, they are."

"Is the treasure in this booth?" Candy asked excitedly.

"Not here," her mother answered. "Do you remember a lady by the name of Mrs. Blanca [BLAHN-kuh] who we met at church?"

"I think so," Candy answered. "Did she use puppets in Sunday School?"

"Yes, she's the one. She has a booth here in the market," her mother said. "Try to find her."

Candy and Timmy took off quickly to look for their new church friend. They hurried from booth to booth.

Five minutes later, Candy shouted, "Here she is! I've found Mrs. Blanca!"

Mother hurried toward the booth gasping for breath. "You are too fast for me, kids."

Mrs. Blanca laughed out loud and greeted them.

"Now, where's the treasure?" Candy asked.

"Look in the java beans," Mrs. Blanca said. "It's OK. Here's a scoop to dig down into the sacks of beans."

Candy took the scoop and dug down into the first burlap sack. "Nothing here," she said.

"Let me try," Timmy said. Mrs. Blanca handed him a scoop, and he dug down into the second sack. "No clue in this one either."

Candy used her scoop on the third burlap sack. The scoop came up full of coffee beans with an envelope sticking out of them. "I found it!" she yelled.

"Read it!" Timmy was jumping up and down.

Candy opened the envelope, pulled out the card, and read:

Clue 3

To solve this clue, think hard each day
Of a favorite game you like to play.
Then find a place that's round about
Where you'll hear a great big cheer and shout.

"Wow! This is another hard clue. Timmy, we'll have to use our gray matter on this one too." She grinned as if she was proud of herself for remembering what gray matter meant.

"But where is the treasure?" Timmy asked.

"I forgot all about the treasure," Candy said.

"I think Mrs. Blanca should tell us," Mother suggested.

"Oh, yes, please tell us," Candy begged.

Mrs. Blanca reached into a sack of java beans and scooped up some in her hands. "These *beans* are a treasure."

"What?" asked Timmy. "How can beans be a treasure?"

"These coffee beans are famous for their flavor," Mrs. Blanca said. "They have a fruit-like taste with a fragrant aroma. It's a favorite coffee of lots of people."

"What's 'fragrant aroma'?" Timmy asked. "We don't have a dictionary here to look up those big words."

Mrs. Caine laughed and told Mrs. Blanca why he said that. Then she answered Timmy's question. "'Fragrant aroma' means a sweet or nice smell."

"I have a question too," Candy said. "What makes the coffee in Cobán so special?"

"The climate up here in the mountains and all the rain makes the difference," Mrs. Blanca said. "Our coffee is shipped all over the world."

"And that's why the java in these sacks is a treasure," Mrs. Caine explained.

"I'll remember this tomorrow morning," Candy said, "when Mom and Dad drink their coffee."

"Not me," Timmy said. "Yuck! I don't like the stuff."

6

The Unexpected Treasure

"Rain, rain, go away. Come again another day." Candy recited a rhyme that her mother taught her. Then she added a line of her own. "I really want to go outside and play, play, play."

"That's very good," her mother said. "You're a poet. But I don't think your poem will stop the rain."

"This rain is terrible," Candy griped. "I'm ready to scream."

"We only have about two and half weeks to go," Rev. Caine said. "Surely you can put up with it that long."

"No treasure hunt," moaned Timmy.

The Caines were eating a breakfast of pancakes before Rev. Caine went to teach his classes.

"Mom, would you play Mexican Train with us?" Candy asked.

"Sure, if you'll help me with the dishes."

"All right. Timmy, I'll dry the dishes and you can put them away."

In a few minutes the dishes were done, and the kitchen was ready for the next meal.

"I'll get the dominoes," said Timmy as he ran to the closet.

In no time at all, the Caines, minus Dad, were happily involved in the game. After drawing dominoes for the fourth round, Candy blurted out, "I don't have any nines! I can't start this round!" She slammed her fist on the table so hard that all the dominoes toppled. Then she pushed back her chair, and it fell over. "I hate this stupid game!" she hollered. She stomped out of the room and slammed her bedroom door.

"Timmy," his mother said, "if you'll put up the dominoes, I'll go talk with Candy. Then you and I will play another game."

"OK," Timmy said. "I'll get the Uno cards."

Mrs. Caine went to Candy's bedroom, opened the door quietly, and walked in. Candy was lying facedown on her bed.

"Candice," her mother said softly but sternly, "why did you get angry just now? You know that is not good behavior."

"I don't care," the girl yelled. "Mexican Train is a dumb game anyway. I'm sick of the game! I'm sick of the rain! And I'm sick of this dumb house!"

"Candy, I'm so disappointed in you. You remember 'J,' don't you?"

"Of course," Candy said. "But right now, Mother, I don't care."

"Then you need a time-out for a while. You have been controlling your anger so well. You haven't been angry like this for several days, and I've been proud of you. But right now, you have made me very sad. You need some time to think about your attitude and behavior."

An hour later, Mrs. Caine went back to Candy. After they prayed together, Candy apologized.

"I promise to do better," Candy said. "I really want Jesus to help me."

"He will. I've told you that many times," her mother said. "Jesus keeps His promises, but He expects you to do your part by working to change too."

✻ ✻ ✻

Four more days of rain passed before the next sunny day. The Caine kids played many games of Mexican Train and Uno. Candy finished her scrapbook about the beautiful market city of Antigua [ahn-TEE-gwuh].

"Fantastic!" yelled Candy, as she got out of bed the next morning. "Look at this beautiful sunshine! I love you, Mr. Sunshine." She pretended to give the sunshine a big hug. As she headed to the kitchen for breakfast, she added, "We can go treasure hunting today."

"Mom, can we go now?" Timmy asked.

"Not until you eat your breakfast," she answered. "You've waited a week, so you can wait another hour."

As the children ate a bowl of Cheerios and some fried plantain, they talked about the last clue.

"Sis, do you know what the clue means?" Timmy asked.

"Well, I think the game the clue refers to may be soccer," Candy answered.

"What makes you think that?"

"Because it is one of our favorite games."

"We like Mexican Train and Uno too," Timmy said.

"But we play those games in our house," Candy explained. "The clue says that we must find a place that is round about where we hear cheers and shouts. That sounds like a place where people play soccer."

"I get it!" Timmy said with excitement. "You are so smart, Sis."

Candy didn't say anything. Instead, she gave her brother a big grin, blew on her fingers, and rubbed them on her left shoulder.

"That's great, Candy," her mother said. "You figured that out with no help from me or your father."

"I just used my gray matter. Five days of monsoon weather gave me lots of time to think."

"What's a 'monsoon'?" asked Timmy.

"Use your noggin," his sister teased him. Then imitating her father, she said, "As Dad would say, 'Why don't you look it up?'"

Timmy got the dictionary. With his mother's help, he found the word and read, "Very heavy rainfall." Then he asked, "Where did you learn that word, Sis?"

"In geography class," she replied.

"Usually, monsoons are found in the southern part of Asia," their mother said. "But sometimes we use the word to exaggerate about heavy rainfall in other parts of the world."

"When are we leaving?" Candy asked.

"As soon as we clean up the kitchen," her mother answered, "and you kids change clothes."

Thirty minutes later, Candy and Timmy hopped into the car with their mother.

"Where are we going?" Candy asked.

"There's a big soccer stadium in Cobán where you will find the next clue and treasure."

"Neat," said Candy.

"Neat," Timmy echoed his sister.

"Mom, is there a soccer game today?" Candy asked.

"I don't think so," her mother answered. "We'll soon find out, won't we?"

After about 15 minutes, Candy yelled, "There it is!" She pointed out the car window.

Timmy was wide-eyed. "It's so big!"

As they drove into the parking lot, Candy was on the edge of her seat. "Look, there are some people playing on the field. Can we watch them, Mom?"

"We'll have to see if this is a game or just a practice," Mrs. Caine answered. "Let's park, and then I'll find out." Mrs. Caine checked with a woman at the gate and learned that the local team was practicing.

"All right, kids, we can go in. There's no cost today."

The three Caines climbed up the steps into the stands. They sat and watched with interest for a few minutes.

Suddenly, Timmy jumped up. "Hey, Mom. I forgot all about the clue and the treasure. Where are they?"

"Yes, tell us," Candy chimed in.

"I want you to walk around the stadium and look for a place where you think a clue might be hidden."

The two kids took off on a run, Timmy right behind his sister. They looked under the wooden steps in the stands. They searched in cans and bottles on the ground. They ran under the stands and looked around. Then they ran back to their mother.

"We can't find it," Candy said. "Can you give us a hint?"

"Look up, look high. The clue you'll spy."

"You're a poet, Mom," Candy said.

"Who do you think wrote the clues?" their mother said with a smile and a wink.

Candy and her brother took off again. They looked up everywhere.

"I think I've found it," yelled Candy. "There's an envelope taped to this pole." She stood on her tiptoes, but she could not reach it. "Mom, come help me."

Mrs. Caine joined her daughter beside the pole and reached up to get the envelope. "I didn't know your father would put it up so high," she said. Then she handed the envelope to Candy who tore it open and took out the clue.

"Read it, read it," Timmy urged.

Candy read aloud:

Clue 4

**To solve this clue, it won't be hard
If you look around in your own yard.
An important clue is a precious stone
That you will find nearby your home.**

"What does that mean?" Candy asked. "Is the treasure back in Guatemala City?"

"It could be," her mother replied, "but maybe not. I want you to use your brains."

"You mean our gray matter," said Candy.

"In our noggins," Timmy added.

"Wonderful," their mother said. "You have learned new words, and you are using them. Both of you are great!"

"Where's the treasure, Mom?" Candy asked. "I don't see a treasure here at the soccer field."

"Let's sit down and I'll tell you."

They climbed the steps into the stands again and sat down. "Do you know what the Alabaster Offering is?" Mrs. Caine asked.

"Sure," said Candy. "It's for buildings on the mission field, right?"

"That's right. And we live in a house in Guatemala City that was built with Alabaster money."

"But what does that have to do with this soccer field?" Candy asked.

"In 1999, the Nazarenes in this country had a big celebration in this soccer stadium. The Alabaster Offering was 50 years old, so the people planned a great big birthday party and invited lots of people. There were about 12,000 people here that day."

"Did they have a birthday cake?" Timmy asked.

"I didn't see any here at the stadium."

"Were you and Dad here?" Candy asked.

"Yes, Candy. That was the year before you were born. Other people came from the United States and some other countries too. But most of the people were from this country. We had four long parades of people marching into this stadium."

"Now, I see why you call this stadium a treasure," Candy said. "It was an unexpected treasure."

"Sis, I know how it could have been a bigger treasure," said Timmy.

"How's that?" his sister asked.

"If they had made a *big* birthday cake to feed all those people," he said. "Yum, yum!"

7
The Precious Treasure

"Another monsoon." Timmy looked as if he were about to cry.

"And another day when we can't go on the treasure hunt," his sister said. "I'll be glad to get back to our home in Guatemala City."

The Caine kids spent another day indoors. They stared out the windows and hoped the rain would stop. They played Mexican Train and Uno until they were tired of them.

"Tony will be here for dinner soon," Mrs. Caine said, "and I need you to help me."

"What do you want me to do?" Candy asked.

"Set the table, please," her mother suggested. "Timmy, please put the trash by the back door. I'll get your dad to take it outside later."

About 20 minutes later, Rev. Caine and Tony arrived from the school. Their clothes were wet from the rain.

"Mmm, something smells good," Jason Caine said. "What are we eating?"

"That's a big surprise." Emma Caine's smile had a bit of mystery. "And the surprise will be ready soon."

Timmy ran to Tony and jumped up to let the man catch him. "I'm glad you are eating with us," Timmy said.

"I'm glad your parents invited me," the soccer player said. "And how is your nose, Miss Candy?"

"It's fine. All the black and blue's gone. See?"

Tony put Timmy down to take a closer look at Candy's nose. "And the scar will be so small that most people will never notice it," Tony said.

Mrs. Caine got their attention. "It's time to eat, so have a seat."

"There you go again," Candy said. "Another rhyme."

"I know," her mother said with a big grin. "I just can't help it."

After Rev. Caine asked the blessing, the family and their guest tackled the feast: chicken with mushrooms and rice, green bean casserole, carrot and pineapple salad, and homemade rolls.

"What's for dessert?" Rev. Caine asked.

"That's a surprise too," his wife replied.

"If it is as good as this food, it will be great. The dinner is scrumptious," Tony said. "Thanks for inviting me."

"What's 'scrumptious'?" Timmy asked. "And, Dad, don't tell me to look it up."

"All right," his father said with a chuckle. "We'll forget the dictionary this time. But what do you think 'scrumptious' means?"

"Does it mean nice?"

"That's a good guess," Rev. Caine said. "Usually, when people say food is 'scrumptious,' they mean it's delicious."

"Very, *very* delicious this time," Tony said. "Your mother is an excellent cook."

"Why, thank you, Tony," she said. "You can come eat with us any time you want."

"I just might," Tony said, as he helped himself to more chicken. "By the way, have you kids figured out the last clue? Your dad told me all about the big treasure hunt."

"It's too hard," Candy said. "The clue says to look in our 'own yard,' nearby our 'home.' That's back in Guatemala City."

"But right now your yard and home are here in Cobán," Tony said. "Does that help?"

"No, because I don't know what the 'precious stone' is," Candy replied. "The only precious stones I know about are diamonds and pearls and rubies."

"There are lots of precious stones," her father said. "I think it's time you kids learn about a very precious stone. Emma, where is that envelope to open only in case of an emergency?"

"In a kitchen cabinet," she replied.

"Well, I think this is an emergency," he said with a wink. "It's time to open the mystery envelope."

Mrs. Caine got the envelope and handed it to her husband. He then passed it on to Candy. "Here, young lady, you can open it and see what it says."

"This is exciting!" she said, as she ripped open the envelope and pulled out a card. She stared at it for a minute and then began to read:

Clue 5
The last clue was puzzling, with that we agree.
This new clue will help solve the big mystery.
Your yard and your home are right here in this place,
And here you will finish your treasure hunt chase.
Go look in the Bible school building nearby,
Inside search around—look low and look high.
The stone alabaster is precious indeed,
So look for a stone jar and you will succeed.

"So, Mom, *you* are the one who put the envelope in my desk," Candy said. "That was tricky."

"I thought that would add a bit of mystery to this treasure hunt," her mother said. "Plus, it's an extra clue to help you find the treasure."

"Can we go look now? Please?" Candy begged. "We can put on our rain ponchos."

"I don't see why not," Father said. "Emma, let's eat the surprise dessert after we get back."

"Sure," Mrs. Caine said. "Let's solve the mystery of the Cobán treasure."

The kids put on their rain ponchos, and their parents and guest got umbrellas. They all hurried to the Bible school building as fast as they could. Inside the two-story school building, the kids started looking for the stone jar.

"Timmy, you look in one classroom," Candy said, "and I'll look in the next one."

"Don't go in any of the offices," Rev. Caine said. "They are off-limits."

The two Caine kids rushed from room to room, but they did not find the stone jar.

"Let's go upstairs," Candy said. "Maybe it's up there."

The kids ran up the steps to the second floor. Tony was right behind them. Candy and Timmy explored every room.

"Where is it, Sis?" Timmy asked. "This is a mystery."

"I don't know," Candy said. "I'm puzzled. Let's sit down and use our noggins."

The sister and brother sat down on the floor in the hall. "Where haven't we looked?" Candy asked.

"Got me," the boy replied.

Tony sat down beside them. "Do you remember that the clue said to 'look low' and 'look high'? Think, kids."

"Mmm, first it says to 'look low.'" Candy scratched her head. "I've got it. It's downstairs."

In a flash, the kids were back on the first floor. They searched and searched, but they did not find the alabaster jar. When Tony caught up with them, he said, "Remember, the clue then said to 'look high.'"

"There it is!" Candy yelled.

"Where?" Timmy asked.

"Up there on that ledge above the front door," she answered. "I don't know why we didn't see it before."

"How are we going to get it down?" Timmy asked. "Dad, do you have a ladder?"

"No ladder needed," Tony said. "Timmy, I'll put you on my shoulders. I think you can reach it. But be careful and hold it tightly."

Soon, Candy was holding the precious treasure. "This white jar is so pretty," she said. "Is this alabaster?"

"Yes," her mother said. "This jar was made with alabaster stone from Italy. Isn't it pretty?"

"But why is this a treasure?" Timmy asked.

"Do you remember when we talked at the soccer field about the Alabaster Offering?"

"Sure," both of the children answered.

"The idea of the Alabaster Offering came from a story in the Bible. A woman broke an alabaster jar and poured perfume on Jesus. Mark tells the story in chapter 14 of his Gospel. We'll read it again before you go to bed tonight."

"I remember that the perfume cost a lot of money, didn't it?" Candy said.

"You're right," her mother replied. "The alabaster jar was made from valuable stone. This woman gave Jesus a precious gift of love. Today, we have Alabaster boxes that we put money in, which help build mission buildings, such as churches, houses, schools, and clinics. When we break open our Alabaster boxes, we give Jesus a special love offering."

"This *place* is a very precious treasure too," Rev. Caine said. "This school building was the first building in the world to be paid for with Alabaster funds."

"This treasure hunt was really fun, Mom," Timmy said. "I'll always remember the treasures we found in Cobán."

"Now I see why this building is a treasure," Candy said. "May I have the alabaster jar, Mom?"

"Yes, I believe that you've earned it," her mother said. "It's yours to keep."

"I'll be careful not to break it," Candy promised. "I want to always remember this alabaster treasure."

"When is the next treasure hunt?" Timmy asked.

"Oh, maybe in 10 years." His mother chuckled and added, "Now let's go eat that surprise dessert."